Praise 1

As our children grow, so do ......, ... Kathleen Nielson's beautifully written book *Prayers of a Parent for Young Adults* is a wonderful guide to help parents pray for a variety of needs. Although young adults may leave our homes, they never leave our hearts. These daily prayers will bless them wherever they may go.

—**Melissa Kruger**, Director of Women's Initiatives, The Gospel Coalition

God invites us to come into his presence in the name of our elder Brother, Jesus, and make our requests known. Much parenting happens on our knees. But what do we say? How do we pray? In *Prayers of a Parent for Young Adults*, Kathleen Nielson provides prayers using Scripture and her own experience. Take this book and learn how to pray by "listening" to Kathleen as she has prayed for her children.

—**Juan R. Sanchez**, Senior Pastor, High Pointe Baptist Church, Austin; Author, *The Leadership Formula: Develop the Next Generation of Leaders in the Church*

Praise for the Prayers of a Parent Series

We love how these beautiful, biblical prayers help us to "pray most earnestly" (1 Thess. 3:10), to "pray without ceasing" (1 Thess. 5:17), and to pray specifically for our own children. Furthermore, pastors should encourage every member to pray for the children of the church and assist them in doing so. This book would be a huge help to that end, for often people are willing to pray but "do not know what to pray for" (Rom. 8:26). For those in congregations that take vows to assist parents in the Christian nurture of their children, we can't imagine a better or more important way of fulfilling their vows than praying for those children from their youth onward.

—**Anne and Ligon Duncan**, Wife, Mother, Christian Educator; Chancellor and CEO, Reformed Theological Seminary

I know of no greater gift that a parent can give to their child than the gift of prayer centered on the gospel. That's why I'm so excited about this project from Kathleen Nielson. Filled with faith, hope, and love, each prayer is accompanied by relevant Scripture and a focused exhortation to help any parent put into words what they long for in their hearts. Having prayed for and with our two daughters for the last two decades, my wife and I look forward to using it!

—**Julius J. Kim**, President, The Gospel Coalition

Kathleen Nielson has coupled scriptural truth with beautifully crafted poetic prayers that bring hope. As a mom, I am encouraged to consider afresh the many ways I must pray for my children. Kathleen helps me with the joyful task by lifting my eyes upward, creating a Word-focused mission of intercession. As a parent (whether natural or spiritual), you too will be challenged in the prayers you pray—prayers that are bound to change not only your children's hearts but yours as well.

—**Blair Linne**, Author; Speaker; Spoken Word Artist

Kathleen Nielson understands the longings of our hearts for the spiritual flourishing of our children. She gives these longings beautiful and Bible-shaped expression. A treasure for every Christian parent!

—**Dane C. Ortlund**, Author, *Gentle and Lowly: The Heart of Christ for Sinners and Sufferers*

There is no greater joy for Christian parents than to hear that their children are walking in the truth. But how do we pray toward that end, day in and day out, through every stage of their lives? I can think of no better guide than this series by Kathleen Nielson—a diligent student of God's Word, a wonderful writer, and a praying mother (and now grandmother). Because these prayers are so Scripture saturated, you can have confidence that you are praying in accord with the will of our good and sovereign God. Take up and read, and pray, and by God's grace you could change your world.

—**Justin Taylor**, Managing Editor, *ESV Study Bible*

Since as parents we have no ability whatsoever to change the hearts of our children, prayer for them is not a spiritual luxury; it is essential. It is an amazing grace to us that God welcomes, hears, and answers our prayers. I know of no other guide to parental prayer like Nielson's tender, insightful, gospel-rich, and loving little book. Read it and you will find yourself praying for new things for your children in new ways than you have before, and as you do, you will grow in affection for your Father and in how you approach him in prayer.

—**Paul David Tripp**, Author, *New Morning Mercies: A Daily Gospel Devotional* and *Parenting: 14 Gospel Principles That Can Radically Change Your Family*

Parenting is important and hard. How do you pray through this complexity? What do you pray when you aren't sure what to say or how to say it? Kathleen Nielson knows the parental spiritual roller-coaster. She's lived it. And prayed through it. This book will give you words to pray and encouragement to ponder as you navigate the issues and challenges of real-world parenting. It helped me. I think it will help you as well.

—**Mark Vroegop**, Lead Pastor, College Park Church, Indianapolis; Author, *Dark Clouds, Deep Mercy: Discovering the Grace of Lament*

Prayers of a Parent
for Young Adults

Prayers of a Parent Series

KATHLEEN NIELSON

Prayers of a Parent for Young Children
Prayers of a Parent for Teens
Prayers of a Parent for Young Adults
Prayers of a Parent for Adult Children

Prayers of a Parent
for Young Adults

Kathleen Nielson

P&R
PUBLISHING
P.O. BOX 817 • PHILLIPSBURG • NEW JERSEY 08865-0817

Printed in the United States of America

Library of Congress Cataloging-in-Publication Data

Names: Buswell Nielson, Kathleen, author.
Title: Prayers of a parent for young adults / Kathleen Nielsen.
Description: Phillipsburg, New Jersey : P&R Publishing, [2021] | Series:
   Prayers of a parent | Summary: "Your child's young adult years are filled with
   joyful opportunity and character-growing challenges. Lift them up to the Lord
   with poetic prayers for their heart, mind, and life of faith."-- Provided by publisher.
Identifiers: LCCN 2021008668 | ISBN 9781629958231 (paperback) | ISBN
   9781629958248 (epub) | ISBN 9781629958255 (mobi)
Subjects: LCSH: Parents--Prayers and devotions. | Young adults--Prayers and
   devotions. | Young adults--Religious life. | Parent and adult
   child--Religious aspects--Christianity.
Classification: LCC BV4529 .B887 2021 | DDC 242/.645--dc23
LC record available at https://lccn.loc.gov/2021008668

For our three sons,
and their three beautiful wives, now like daughters,
and our grandchildren, eight so far—
what amazing gifts from God.
I love praying for you!

Contents

CONTENTS

Introduction

How being a parent makes one pray—without ceasing! The prayers of this volume reach out to the Lord for our young adult children: from late teens into early adulthood. In these years, children leap into independence, pursue life callings, and often leave home. Prayer has been crucial from the beginning, but as these young adults begin to find their own pathways, we parents even more deeply understand the importance and the comfort of praying for our children. How amazing to think that Christian parents can keep reaching out in prayer to God our Father, who has shown his love to us in his own Son—and who gives us his Holy Spirit to help us pray, according to his Word.

These prayers have grown from my heart through years of praying for three sons—and now for their growing families. I know that you parents (and grandparents, and aunts and uncles, and spiritual mothers and fathers!) will surely pray for your children in your own words and with your own specific praises and petitions. My hope is that these prayers might mingle profitably with yours, as we all lift up the next generations to the Lord who knows and loves them perfectly.

These prayers grow out of the Scriptures; each is printed

with a brief related Bible passage and reflects that passage in its content. What confidence, that when we don't know how to pray for our children, the Spirit and the Word guide and help us. Just as the Scriptures show us Jesus Christ at the very center, so these prayers aim to focus on Jesus—his love, his work of salvation on our behalf, his glory, his blessed rule in every area of our lives, his coming again.

The prayers apply to sons and daughters both; they alternate, but any of them can easily be changed by switching the pronouns appropriately. Please note: the prayers are written in one parent's voice, although they can certainly be prayed by parents together. Parents, please know that these prayers, as they focus on our children, inevitably focus often on us parents too. Prayer stretches our hearts in all kinds of ways.

Let us pray!

Kathleen Nielson

Our soul waits for the LORD;
*   he is our help and our shield.*
For our heart is glad in him,
*   because we trust in his holy name.*
Let your steadfast love, O LORD, be upon us,
*   even as we hope in you. (Ps. 33:20–22)*

How beautifully the psalmist teaches us to wait on the Lord and hope in the Lord—and how crucial are these lessons in relation to parenting!

We begin this volume with a psalm that turns us toward true hope. These young adult years are the ones in which we might hope to see the fruit of our labors in our children. But it is good for us to step back and remember where our hope ultimately lies: in the unfailing faithfulness and steadfast love of our sovereign God who sent his only Son to save us. We can trust in his holy name, all the days of our lives and of our children's lives.

Of Thanks and Trust

O Lord my God, in you I rest my soul,
for only you are my help and shield;
my heart is glad in you.
As I fill up the years with prayers
for my dear child,
I trust you,
all because of who you are,
O Lord my God,
the God of steadfast love
who gave your only Son for our salvation.

I'm praying always that your steadfast love
would be upon my child,
both now and evermore.
I tell you, Lord, in faith,
my trust and hope lie not
in how, according to your providence,
you send the answer to my prayers;
I hope in you.

O Lord my God,
I thank you that you hear my prayers.
I thank you that you've granted me the blessing large
of showing off your steadfast love
before my child,
imperfectly, but by your grace.
May I be an ever-faithful witness,
even as I pray,
and as I wait and hope in you.

May our sons in their youth
  be like plants full grown,
our daughters like corner pillars
  cut for the structure of a palace. (Ps. 144:12)

We sometimes say we would like to keep them young and close, but we know we're aiming for much more than that. We're aiming to see them grow into women and men of mature faith, ready to go out and serve the God who made them.

We're aiming, as Psalm 144 pictures it, for sons who are like full-grown plants, sturdy and fruitful, and for daughters who are like the pillars of a palace, strong and noble. We're aiming for children full of spiritual life and strength, who will play their parts well in showing and sharing that life and strength, all through the power of Jesus Christ our risen Savior and Lord.

May we pray for the maturity of our children with the kind of faith-filled vision that Scripture encourages in us.

For her maturity I pray: see Ephesians 4:11–16.

For Strong Faith

For her maturity I pray, O Lord—
that she would grow not just in body strong
but even more in soul. Please never cease to grow in her
a soul of faith that presses on in knowing you
and building up your church
and aiming for the day she'll see your face.

No longer a child tossed about
by every new idea, every wind of doctrine,
may she live as one who's planted firm
among your people, Lord,
all united by your breathed-out Word
and growing up in every way together
into Christ our head.

With strength of soul give her humility,
daily acknowledgement of sins and failings
which, I pray, will take her only, always, to the cross
where Christ our Savior died for us;
may she not forget that cross,
and not forget the empty tomb
that shows Christ risen, conquering death,
the living Lord of our salvation.

Father, be her guide as she walks onward, strong
because she's looking to her risen Savior,
strengthened by your Spirit,
aiming for the day she sees you face to face.

Again Jesus spoke to them, saying, "I am the light of the world. Whoever follows me will not walk in darkness, but will have the light of life." (John 8:12)

Reading this, you may be a believing parent who grieves over your grown child's unbelief and who yearns for God to invade that child's heart. Nothing makes us yearn more.

And nothing makes us turn more fervently to the truths on which we stake our lives: God's sovereignty, God's love shown in his Son, God's power to accomplish all his perfect will.

God sent his Son, who is the light of the world. Let us pray that God will shine that light into this child's heart.

"Let there be light": see Genesis 1:3. *You sent your light*: see John 1:4–5.

For an Unbelieving Child

Break your light upon my child's heart,
O Lord who only said, "Let there be light,"
and there was light.
You sent your light into this world,
a light that shines in darkness
and is not ever overcome.

O shine the light of Jesus in his heart,
merciful Father, by your Spirit,
that my child may believe.

Thank you, sovereign God,
that you hold my beloved child in your hand.
You always have, and all my efforts—
sometimes feeble or foolish, sometimes wise—
you know, you use, according to your plan.
I know that you are sovereign
and that you are good,
and so I still my yearning soul before your throne.

In you is life, fully revealed and given in your Son
who died for sinners who deserve that death,
who rose that sinners who believe might live.
Enlarge my heart, I pray,
to yearn for many sinners to believe and live.

But now I stop to pray again,
and I will pray again, O Lord of life:
please shine the light of Jesus in his heart,
that my child may believe.

For the LORD gives wisdom;
from his mouth come knowledge and understanding.
(Prov. 2:6)

They will probably be reading a lot in these years. Hopefully these young adults will make their way through many whole books along with all the shorter snippets and articles and blogs. And hopefully one book, the Bible, will be opened and read again and again.

We all know the temptation to let other words crowd out God's Word. In our interconnected world, we (younger and older alike) often begin the morning and mark the segments of our day by checking on words—whether messages from friends and family or perhaps items of interesting news. More words are always waiting.

In the midst of all the other words, it is the Bible that will give us wisdom, direct from God's mouth. These are the words of life. May our children know this, and may they discipline themselves (and delight themselves) in reading and studying the Scriptures regularly and deeply.

For Delight in God's Word

From your mouth, Lord, let her receive
the words of wisdom that will give her life.
May she not put your Book aside, as one she's read,
but may she lean in daily toward the breath of God
that warms her soul, lights her imagination,
gives her knowledge of the one true God.

May she delight to hear your voice, O Father;
through it may she grow to know you,
by your Spirit, through your Son.

As she sifts through a world of words,
a myriad of voices,
give her understanding, Lord,
discernment growing from the Word
that's planted ever deeper in her,
flavoring her tastes and likes and loves,
showing her you,
and all the rest in light of you.

May she read your Word not only alone
but regularly in the company of saints
who live to love and follow Jesus,
and whose zeal to know him through the Word
will pull her on when she needs heartening.
May those saints teach her to hearten others
through the words of life that come from your own mouth.

May she delight to hear your voice, O merciful Lord.

But when the fulness of time had come, God sent forth his Son, born of woman, born under the law, to redeem those who were under the law, so that we might receive adoption as sons. And because you are sons, God has sent the Spirit of his Son into our hearts, crying, "Abba! Father!" So you are no longer a slave, but a son, and if a son, then an heir through God. (Gal. 4:4–7)

The role of a human parent is a privileged one, one to treasure. Its blessing, however, reflects a much greater blessing, one we're meant to pass on in our parenting: the fatherhood of God.

The Bible reveals God as the ultimate parent—sometimes pictured as a mother and most often called our Father. He is the source of life, salvation, security, joy, hope. He is a believer's "Abba! Father!"—all that even the best earthly father only dimly pictures. And he is the Father we long for our children to know and love. As earthly parents, we get to point our children to the heavenly parent.

May we send forth our children as children of the heavenly Father.

For Identity in You

May my child know himself to be
a child of you, my heavenly Father.
Never just mine, but always yours,
please let him celebrate adoption
in your family, crying by your Spirit
"Abba! Father!"

Sometimes I think of what he might receive
as heir within our earthly family,
as we take the greatest care for generations
still to come. And yet,
these temporary goods,
seeming however great or little,
glimmer like a firefly caught in a child's hand
next to the brilliant shining sun
of our inheritance in Christ
that will not ever dim or fade.

Please let him revel even now
as your adopted child
in that amazing joy
of calling you his "Abba! Father!"
Let him walk forward
in the confidence of one redeemed
by faith in your own Son who died
and in whom we are brought into your family
all by your grace, and all as sons forever loved.

May my child live as your child, Father,
lifting up your name forever.

Do you not know that you are God's temple and that God's Spirit dwells in you? If anyone destroys God's temple, God will destroy him. For God's temple is holy, and you are that temple. (1 Cor. 3:16–17)

Or do you not know that your body is a temple of the Holy Spirit within you, whom you have from God? You are not your own, for you were bought with a price. So glorify God in your body. (1 Cor. 6:19–20)

First Corinthians 3:16–17 addresses the *plural* "you"—speaking to the Corinthian church, God's "temple" where his Spirit dwells and where impurity must not dwell. First Corinthians 6:19 addresses the *singular* "you"—speaking to individual believers, each one a "temple of the Holy Spirit" that must be kept pure from sexual sin. Both the corporate body of Christ and a believer's individual body are called a *temple* where the Holy Spirit dwells.

What was true for the Corinthian believers is true for us today: we believers are God's temple, corporately and individually. What a wonder! And what fodder for prayer—for the church, for individuals who are part of that church, and certainly for our children walking into adulthood, facing all kinds of fleshly temptations. By God's grace they carry within them God's own presence, his Spirit, making their very bodies his temple.

For a Body Pure and Holy

Such holiness, Lord, linked to and living in our bodies . . .
let her by faith grasp more and more the truth
that as your child she is a walking, breathing temple,
filled with your own Spirit sent to us your people
by the risen Christ, to claim us, seal us as your own,
body and soul, forever.

Please let her treasure well the body knit by you
while she was in the womb, designed by you
to bring you glory. May she see and celebrate
your good creation of us, male and female;
may she find her place according to your plan
among your people made to rule and fill the earth,
made to worship you together, as a church
of men and women who unite to make a temple
where you dwell, both now and in eternity,
when we in glorified and resurrected bodies
will forever bring you glory, our Creator and Redeemer God.

Even as we pray to keep the church, Christ's body,
pure and holy, by the power of your Spirit,
so I pray my child will keep her body
pure and holy, set apart for you, O loving Father.
Please empower her by your Spirit
to resist temptation of the flesh;
help her resist the draw of sins against her body;
may she know and not forget
that her own flesh is not a treasure she is meant to own—
but that her whole self, body and soul,
is made and known and bought with a price by you.

*I hope to come to you soon, but I am writing these things to
you so that, if I delay, you may know how one ought to behave
in the household of God, which is the church of the living God,
a pillar and buttress of the truth. (1 Tim. 3:14–15)*

The apostle Paul gives young Pastor Timothy a wonderful and
personal name for the church: it is the "household of God." It's
where we live, as those redeemed by Christ. God's people make
the ultimate home, the ultimate family, for a believer; as we'll
note later, a church congregation is full of spiritual mothers and
fathers and sisters and brothers (see 1 Tim. 5:1–2).

From one perspective, it's humbling to admit that our children need more mothers and fathers and sisters and brothers
than can be found at home. From a bigger perspective, it's ultimately comforting: we parents give our children all we can, by
God's grace—and then the household of God fills in all the
gaps, throughout their lives and forever!

The body of Christ is our forever family. Let's pray that our
children learn well to live in and love the family of God.

For Love of the Church

Wherever he makes his home, dear Father,
for a little or a longer while,
let him find home among your people.
Give him a longing deep and instinct strong
to find a family of faith
that loves the Savior,
clearly speaks the Word of truth,
and follows the command
to love their neighbors as themselves.

Make him at home among your people, Lord.
Please let him yearn to sit and sing
among the children
and the white-haired ones,
feeling all the fullness of your body,
knowing this is final family.

Among your people,
let him know and show the strength
yet not the arrogance of youth;
may he be quiet to listen,
ready with open heart to feed
on your Word preached.

Even in his youth
please may he serve and love and teach your family well;
among your people give him fathers, mothers, sisters, brothers
for whom he would give his life
and with whom he can make a home
and be at home, with you, forever.

So flee youthful passions and pursue righteousness, faith, love, and peace, along with those who call on the Lord from a pure heart. (2 Tim. 2:22)

Surrounding voices often call young people to *follow* youthful passions, not *flee* them. The apostle Paul not only calls young Timothy to flee the naturally strong passions of our sinful hearts (such as lust or anger); he calls him to pursue a completely different direction, living to please the Lord who has saved us.

Paul pictures this fleeing and pursuing as done not alone but "along with those who call on the Lord from a pure heart." Even as we pray for righteousness, faith, love, and peace in our children, we can pray that they would be surrounded by saints (including ourselves!) who are by God's grace pursuing these qualities. We can pray that, as part of the body of Christ and by the power of Christ, they would be transformed more and more into the image of Christ.

For Fleeing and Pursuing

Let her not be content to stay, along the path,
making a home before she's home,
forgetting what lies ahead,
or even turning back to grasp
what should be put away and left far, far behind.
In comfort or discomfort,
may she press ahead within her soul,
led and walking by your Spirit, sometimes running,
to pursue the righteousness and faith and love
that grow in one made new by faith
in Christ who died and rose to lead the way
toward all that we pursue
until we see him face to face.

With heart made pure by Christ our Savior,
may she flee the passions that would soil his name
and break his Word
and cloud communion with you, Lord.
Help her turn and run not just away
but full ahead toward you,
compelled to follow where you lead,
all by your grace.

Thank you, dear Father, that she need not run alone
but in the company of those purehearted saints
who are your children,
who call on your name,
who follow you wholeheartedly
until the end, and evermore.

May the Lord grant mercy to the household of Onesiphorus,
for he often refreshed me and was not ashamed of my chains,
but when he arrived in Rome he searched for me earnestly
and found me—may the Lord grant him to find mercy from
the Lord on that day!—and you well know all the service he
rendered at Ephesus. (2 Tim. 1:16–18)

Friendships can be an amazing window into the heart of God. Love, joy, help, self-sacrifice . . . God's grace and God's nature are revealed in the bonds that grow between friends.

Our young adult children are increasingly distanced from us parents in various ways—and that is natural. In these years especially, how good to pray that they would find and grow rich friendships in which they would both glimpse and live out the heart of God.

For Friendships

May you make him the friend who's not ashamed
of his friend's chains, invisible or visible;
the friend who is not slow to search and find
and help his friend in need;
the friend who will refresh another,
often at his own expense, but never keeping count.

May you bring friends his way to teach him friendship—
those who refresh him, never looking round
to see who's watching, measuring, critiquing,
rather simply giving of themselves to love and serve,
even laying their lives down, all for a friend.

May his friends pray mercy on his head
and on his house, with thankful hearts
for such a friend.
And may his friends and he
look to you, Lord, for mercy,
all through Christ our merciful Savior.
May your infinite mercy pierce us, young or old,
change us, make us merciful friends
like Christ who searched and found us
even in our chains,
and brought us perfect help.

And may my child now grown
keep growing to resemble Christ his Savior,
serving, loving well his friends.

I acknowledged my sin to you,
   and I did not cover my iniquity;
I said, "I will confess my transgressions to the LORD,"
   and you forgave the iniquity of my sin.

Therefore let everyone who is godly
   offer prayer to you at a time when you may be found;
surely in the rush of great waters,
   they shall not reach him.
You are a hiding place for me;
   you preserve me from trouble;
   you surround me with shouts of deliverance. (Ps. 32:5–7)

As we pray, we pray that our children will pray—and not rote prayers, or prayers for others to hear, or prayers only for help, but rather regular prayers of personal communion with God our Father through the Lord Jesus and with the help and ministry of the Holy Spirit.

What a wonder, to talk to our Father about our children's talking to him. What confidence, to know the Lord hears our prayers.

For a Heart to Pray

May the first-person pronouns of the psalms
come from her mouth and from her heart, O Lord.
May she pour out these words herself
and know the meaning of confessing sin before you,
celebrating your forgiveness—saying it and singing it
with confidence that you know and hear.

May she sense deep the urgency of offering prayer
to you our Father, you who by your grace are found by us
in Christ your Son who bore our sin.
Please let prayer not be her last resort in trouble;
rather let her know the goodness
of that daily hiding place
where we by faith commune with you,
where we can hear your voice and talk to you,
helped by your Spirit,
and where you keep us safe from evil and from harm.

May she delight to pray among your people,
joining psalms and hymns, praises, petitions,
all in chorus with a family who loves and needs you,
who together seeks you in the ordinary days
and in the days of fiery trials
when we lift each other up to you, O Lord,
and you in mercy hear our prayers.

May she hear your call to pray,
and may she know the joy
of saying in your presence, Lord,
"You are a hiding place for me."

Each one must give as he has decided in his heart, not reluctantly or under compulsion, for God loves a cheerful giver. And God is able to make all grace abound to you, so that having all sufficiency in all things at all times, you may abound in every good work. (2 Cor. 9:7–8)

Human generosity flows most freely in the context of God's outpouring of grace toward us—as in Paul's mention of "all grace" abounding to us. We have been given stores of riches in Christ. Think of Paul's words in Romans 8:32: "He who did not spare his own Son but gave him up for us all, how will he not also with him graciously give us all things?"

Let's pray that our children would know the ultimately cheerful heart of a generous giver fully provided for by the God who gave his own Son to save us.

For Generosity

The more he has to give, Lord,
let him give, with readiness and cheer,
not putting trust in what remains,
but always conscious of the never-ending store of grace
abounding from our heavenly Father
who gave his own Son
and who along with him gives us all things,
abundantly, sufficiently, and without end.

Open his heart and hand to those you've given him,
not just his family in the flesh
but his eternal family—
both ones familiar, close,
and ones who carry the gospel far away
to grow this family and see good news
spread all across this globe.

Whether it be near or far,
a neighbor or a ministry
in need of time or prayer
or expertise or money,
let him give, Lord, from his heart.
Let him grow and bend toward generosity.
Give him a spirit full of cheer and full of you;
may ones who find themselves receiving
get a taste, a whiff of heavenly feasts
that waken joy and draw them
to a God whose plenteous blessings
overflow to us in Christ his Son.

To this end we always pray for you, that our God may make you worthy of his calling and may fulfill every resolve for good and every work of faith by his power, so that the name of our Lord Jesus may be glorified in you, and you in him, according to the grace of our God and the Lord Jesus Christ. (2 Thess. 1:11–12)

What will my child choose to study or to train for? What jobs will be available? How will he or she juggle various plans for church, family, work, and civic involvement? Watching our children find their way makes us parents pray.

In the midst of praying specifically for all these various callings, may we pray that the one calling of God to faith in Jesus Christ might be clear and preeminent in our child's life. May that calling shape all the other callings, as they come and go.

From personal experience, we know this is a prayer that never ends as the years go by.

The way, the truth, the life: see John 14:6.

For Clear Calling

O God who calls us,
let her hear your call to faith, I pray,
and let her follow faithfully her Savior,
knowing you have known and gifted her,
knowing that she lives and moves
as one who has been called by you
to glorify the name of Jesus.

Let every calling of her life
find place within your gracious, saving call;
may paths of family, work, and service all
be channeled and be lighted
by the glorious One who is the way, the truth, the life;
may all her works be works of faith
that glorify the name of Jesus.

As she traces out the trails you put before her,
may she pray and strive to follow straight and strong,
but may she always think about your providential hand
establishing her steps and ordering her ways
for purposes she may not understand
until she's finished every calling you will grant her—
granted all to glorify the name of Jesus.

Give her wisdom at each turning, Lord I pray
(as I look back and trace the winding
trails on which you've led me).
May you grow her vision for large callings;
may you pour out grace for ones that seem so small;
may you grant her open ears to hear your call
to glorify the name of Jesus.

*They read from the book, from the Law of God, clearly, and
they gave the sense, so that the people understood the reading.
(Neh. 8:8)*

Nehemiah 8 describes a worship gathering of the remnant of
God's people who had returned from exile to their land. As the
books of Moses were read aloud, the Levites moved among
the people, further reading and then explaining God's Word so
that the people understood it. In the end, the people went their
way rejoicing, "because they had understood the words that
were declared to them" (v. 12).

Understanding words . . . it's what God created us to do. Let's
pray that our grown children will do it well and know the joy
of it—first and foremost as they take in God's inspired Word.

The mind of Christ: see 1 Corinthians 2:14–16.

For Reading and Study

On his shelf and in his mind,
may your Word be at front,
the one he reaches for,
the one most worn, most known, most loved.

May you bring friends and teachers who are wise
and who lead him to read, to seek clear meaning
and to understand the sense of Scripture, book by book,
in ways that bring both light and joy.

In that bright light may he seek truth in all he reads and studies,
truth and beauty that originate in you, Creator God,
Redeeming Lord who wakens and transforms our minds
so we can somehow have the mind of Christ our Savior.

Please let him shine the light of truth on what is false,
on any words that contradict your perfect law,
on writing that would dull our love for what is beautiful—
for what is Christ, our all in all.

May he read deep and wide and well, led by your Spirit,
with ability according to your measure and gifting
to make sense of words that unlock worlds—and may he share
the joy of understanding words according to your Word.

Do you see a man who is wise in his own eyes?
  There is more hope for a fool than for him. (Prov. 26:12)

Humility is an elusive quality to pray for . . . when can we say we truly have it or fully understand it? Who of us would ever say that?

But we might say we're *learning* humility, as we learn more of God and as we see ourselves more clearly in light of him. And we can pray that our children would be learning it—that they would clearly see not only their own sin but also their immense eternal value as created and redeemed children of a glorious and loving God.

As we pray for humility for our children, in the Lord's presence we learn more about humility ourselves. May the learning never end.

For Humility

Would you let her see herself as you see her,
dear Father who looks down on us from heaven?
Make her strong and wise, and make her humble,
with a heart that comes to you with no entitlement,
never a proud defense,
but childlike, needy, hungry for what only you provide.

Would you give her eyes for others as you see them,
dear Father who sees deep into our needy souls?
Let her resist comparing, envying, or setting herself above,
as she remembers Christ who came down low
to serve us sinners;
may she humble herself and follow in his way.

Would you set her gaze on you in all your glory,
dear Father who has shown yourself in Christ your Son?
In your light may she see herself as blessed beyond imagining
both to receive eternal and abundant life
and to proclaim it humbly—
wisely, strongly, humbly, for your glory alone.

Share in suffering as a good soldier of Christ Jesus. (2 Tim. 2:3)

Writing to Timothy, the apostle Paul describes his own willing suffering for the sake of the gospel and encourages Timothy to be willing to suffer as well, "as a good soldier of Christ Jesus."

Some of our suffering comes as we believers faithfully live and proclaim the good news of salvation in Jesus; some comes simply as a result of living in this fallen world, waiting for the return of the Lord Jesus. In all cases, Paul's exhortation to Timothy rings out instructively: *share in suffering* (in fellowship with others) *as a good soldier of Jesus* (trusting and obeying Jesus our Lord and Savior to the end).

I would rather just pray for my child's suffering to go away. *Lord, help me learn to pray that he or she would share in suffering as a good soldier of Christ Jesus.*

To know the fellowship of Christ: see Philippians 3:10.

For Strength to Suffer Well

He will meet suffering, Lord, I know,
and so I pray acknowledging your good and providential hand
that leads him where you know he needs to go
to learn and to become all you intend for him
and in him, for the glory of your Son.

May he meet suffering as a faithful soldier of Christ Jesus,
not trusting in his own great strength and wisdom,
and not aiming for a victory that is his, for all to see,
but rather following his Lord, his Savior,
aiming with an undivided heart to bring all honor to his name.

Let him know comfort in his suffering, Lord, I pray;
let hands and prayers of family in the faith come round him,
joining in the journey, calling him not only to stand firm
but to press hard ahead, not shrinking back,
knowing the battle against evil has been won.

In sufferings common to our fallen world,
or sufferings that come because he speaks the name of Christ
and will not compromise the gospel truth,
please give him Spirit-led faith to see your hand,
patience to persevere through pain,
and joy, to know the fellowship of Christ who died for him.

Folly is a joy to him who lacks sense,
  but a man of understanding walks straight ahead.
    (Prov. 15:21)

We parents tend to be quite good at imagining (and perhaps worrying about) the kinds of folly into which our children can so easily fall.

Better to spend time asking the Lord to help them learn how to walk the path of wisdom and not of folly—straight ahead, not turning to the right or to the left (see Prov. 4:25–27).

And better to replace worry with prayerful trust. Our good and merciful Lord sees our children and sovereignly lays out their paths.

In whom are hidden wisdom's treasures: see Colossians 2:1–3.

For Not Folly but Wisdom

May I put forth the simplest prayer, O Lord,
that you would keep her far from folly?

Keep her, I pray, from morning folly
that would flood her mind with her own wants and plans
without the prayer and seeking you that steers her straight.

Keep her, I pray, from daytime folly
that would call her from her work before it's done
or tell her of the pleasure of a seeming small deceit
that will allow her to be done, or to be first, or to be happy.

Keep her, I pray, from folly that so often fills the nighttime
              hours;
from folly that would disregard the need for sleep;
from folly of a foolish friend who calls some evil good;
from folly of a thoughtless act that brings a moment's pleasure
and a long regret.

Help her to listen deeply, daily, to the voice of wisdom;
may she look to Christ in whom are hidden wisdom's treasures
given to us freely, bought with his own blood
for us who wander far, so far from you.
May she daily repent, and daily turn,
and daily walk the path that stretches straight ahead
to joy, with you.

And he said to them, "The harvest is plentiful, but the labor-ers are few. Therefore pray earnestly to the Lord of the harvest to send out laborers into his harvest. Go your way; behold, I am sending you out as lambs in the midst of wolves." (Luke 10:2–3)

Do you not say, "There are yet four months, then comes the harvest"? Look, I tell you, lift up your eyes, and see that the fields are white for harvest. Already the one who reaps is receiving wages and gathering fruit for eternal life, so that sower and reaper may rejoice together. (John 4:35–36)

As I've relished interacting with many Christian young people who are hearing the call to ministry or missions, it's been clear that one weighty factor in such a young person's thinking is often the attitude of parents.

Every situation is different. Wise parental counsel is wonder-ful and crucial to offer at the right time—including questions and concerns, when appropriate. But it is good to be asking ourselves as parents whether our hearts are truly open to God's plans for our children. Are we not just open but eager, praying for our children to serve the Lord wherever he calls them?

We and our children need prayer in these matters.

For a Heart for the Harvest

Earnestly I pray to you, Lord of the harvest,
that you would send out laborers into the fields
that are so ripe for reaping—
and in my prayers I give again my child to you.

Would you give him passion for the harvest,
prayers unceasing for the growing fruit of eternal life,
vision for the nations where the laborers are few—
and, should it be your will, let him answer your call and go.

May your church together hear your call;
unsettle us with urgency
so that we pray, and give, and go—
and with your people, Lord, unsettle him with harvest need.

May we hear not only duty's voice
but that of Jesus whom we love
who calls us all to look and see the fruit that is to come—
Lord, let him hear your voice, and follow you.

As he discerns your callings, Father God,
please motivate his heart (and mine) with harvest joy
to know the path he walks even today
leads to that final Day of gathering before your throne.

"But a Samaritan, as he journeyed, came to where he was, and when he saw him, he had compassion. He went to him and bound up his wounds, pouring on oil and wine. Then he set him on his own animal and brought him to an inn and took care of him. And the next day he took out two denarii and gave them to the innkeeper, saying, 'Take care of him, and whatever more you spend, I will repay you when I come back.' Which of these three, do you think, proved to be a neighbor to the man who fell among the robbers?" He said, "The one who showed him mercy." And Jesus said to him, "You go, and do likewise." (Luke 10:33–37)

When a man walking along a road was stripped, beaten, and left half dead by robbers, both a priest and a Levite passed by on the other side. But a Samaritan showed mercy.

What a huge blessing for us to pray for our children as they hear Jesus's command to go and do likewise. They may find ways and places to show God's mercy that are different from the ways and places we've known. The world around us is ever changing, but the nature of God's mercy does not change. God has mercy on sinners who believe in his Son, and those redeemed sinners then mercifully minister in the name of Jesus to the bodies and souls of those God puts in their path.

May our children know God's mercy and minister mercifully—in and through the Lord Jesus Christ.

For a Heart of Mercy

O holy God, please let my child give of herself
without delusion as to her own righteousness
apart from your great mercy through your Son,
who bore our sin and clothes us in his righteousness
when we bow down in faith.

Let her not ever hold herself apart, as somehow better;
may she know her need, and may she have quick eyes
to see the needs of others you put in her path,
who to a person share that sickness caught by sinners
and whose help is only in your Son our Savior.

May she not be afraid to move in close to need,
to be exposed to this disease we recognize
and share, and for which we have met the cure.
With every open hand let there be opening of her heart
to act and speak and love like Jesus your beloved Son.

May I be thankful in my heart to see her move
toward need or sickness I've not known,
or dangers that might seize my mind as I lay down to sleep;
allay my fears for her, O Father God; may I rejoice
to see her following your Son.

Please send her where she'll learn just what it means
to love and long for mercy deep, not outer show.
Make her your merciful servant, living with a heart of thanks
for your amazing grace in saving her, a sinner,
through your Son who calls her to show mercy in his name.

Wash yourselves; make yourselves clean;
  remove the evil of your deeds from before my eyes;
cease to do evil,
  learn to do good;
seek justice,
  correct oppression;
bring justice to the fatherless,
  plead the widow's cause. . . .

Zion shall be redeemed by justice,
  and those in her who repent, by righteousness. (Isa. 1:16–
    17, 27)

All around us today are the "fatherless" and "widows" who have experienced the kind of oppression our Father in heaven hates. Isaiah's call to bring justice to such oppressed ones rings in our ears.

This call takes on full meaning in the context of all of Isaiah's words, which embed the call for justice in an acknowledgment of our need for God's ultimate justice—in fact, for God in his justice and righteousness to redeem us sinners who repent before him.

Without remembering the Suffering Servant Isaiah foresees (see Isaiah 53), without making our way to the cross where Jesus Christ suffered God's just wrath in our place, we cannot begin to understand justice. Starting there, we begin, and we earnestly pray.

For Practicing Justice

Justice is what you desire, Lord,
what you talk about and what you command—
and so we pray for justice.
I pray that my child will have open ears
to hear your call to seek and bring your justice
to the fatherless and to the widow,
to the ones whom those in wealth and power
step upon and leave behind.

But, Lord, you call us first to wash ourselves,
before we rush to do some good—
to clean the evil from ourselves,
we who think we can wield wealth or power.
And so, O Holy God, we bow, and we repent.
May my child bow before you,
knowing his own need for washing,
knowing, too, your promise to redeem us
by your perfect justice
full-displayed in Christ your perfect Servant,
our Redeemer who bore all our sin
and all your wrath, on our behalf,
upon that cross.

Send my child to practice justice that flows forth from you,
O just Redeemer, loving Holy One.
May he bring fatherless to comfort,
finally to you, the final comfort.
May he bring those who have been left alone
to fellowship, to feasting, hosted by your Son.

And do not fear those who kill the body but cannot kill the soul. Rather fear him who can destroy both soul and body in hell. Are not two sparrows sold for a penny? And not one of them will fall to the ground apart from your Father. But even the hairs of your head are all numbered. Fear not, therefore; you are of more value than many sparrows. (Matt. 10:28–31)

There is only One to fear, our Father in heaven, and his wrath has been turned away from us by his own Son who bore it.

As we fear our heavenly Father with loving reverence and obedience, we can give him our children and ask that he would teach them to fear him, and nothing but him. May they learn to fear him as their Father through faith in his Son.

What a release from all earthly fears. May we and may our children know this release.

For Facing Fears

It's you, all you, to meet her in her fears, O Father—
not that it was ever anything but you, finally you,
who calmed and satisfied her when she was afraid.
But now as she walks forward into life
(and as I practice peace in opening my hands, again),
I pray that she would learn how to allay her earthly fears
in light of you her heavenly Father
whom she fears above all else,
the one who holds her soul and body in your hand
for all eternity.

Help her seek you, when she's afraid—
whether of failure in an overwhelming task,
or scorn from those who have no heart for you,
or physical danger, even death—
whatever fears she faces, may she look to you her Father,
knowing that not even one small sparrow falls upon the ground
apart from you,
who value her much more than many sparrows.

O Lord, I pray that you would shield her from harm;
may you protect her, too, from threatening fears
that might make her feet stumble, halt, or turn
from the straight path you call her to pursue
in faith, with eyes ahead and fixed on you.

Let her fear you,
and, fearing you, dear Father,
may she reject unworthy fears;
may she with every step learn trust in you.

And if your hand causes you to sin, cut it off. It is better for you to enter life crippled than with two hands to go to hell, to the unquenchable fire. And if your foot causes you to sin, cut it off. It is better for you to enter life lame than with two feet to be thrown into hell. And if your eye causes you to sin, tear it out. It is better for you to enter the kingdom of God with one eye than with two eyes to be thrown into hell, "where their worm does not die and the fire is not quenched." (Mark 9:43–48)

I've heard it said that one of the marks of maturity is connecting this present moment to all the moments to come. That makes sense—especially in the spiritual realm, where believing in the great, now-invisible realities to come makes all the difference in how we live right now.

Heaven . . . hell . . . the glorious face of the risen Lord Jesus . . . we shall see it all soon. Give us eyes of faith now, Lord, and give our children eyes of faith now, so they might live with the long view.

All disarmed and shamed: see Colossians 2:13–15. *We will fully be like him*: see 1 John 3:1–3.

For the Long View

Give him the long view, Lord;
let him believe that beyond what he sees and does
right now
lie vast invisible realms that stretch eternally,
connecting his own story with a larger one,
a grand one, that involves a heavenly throne
and hosts of angels and archangels,
and the fallen Satan and his followers
all disarmed and shamed by Jesus at the cross
and in his glorious resurrection,
and yet fighting still, until the story's end
when Jesus Christ will come again in glory and in final
        judgment.

In the midst of such a story, let him hate the sin
that befits hell, not heaven;
let him believe, and let him live the life
Christ died to give to all believers,
with a heart made new
and by the Spirit putting sin away
and growing to be more and more like Christ,
until that Day when we will fully be like him,
for we will see him as he is.

May he live this day fully alert to that one,
knowing with a sense of joy and holy fear
that he is living in your grand and glorious story,
privileged to glimpse the landscapes large
of heaven and hell.

But seek first the kingdom of God and his righteousness, and
all these things will be added to you. (Matt. 6:33)

The kingdom of God and the kingdom of the internet make a strange juxtaposition. Inevitably, we all spend a great deal of time online—for entertainment, for information, for work, for socializing, and even sometimes for worship. Rising generations have grown up utterly comfortable living a great percentage of their waking hours there; they are at home online.

May the home that most deeply draws our children (and us) be God's kingdom. May our children (and may we) long to live in God's presence. May they (and may we) seek him first and see all the rest in light of him.

For Wisdom in Cyberspace

So many worthy things to seek
in that always-expanding virtual world—
a word's clear meaning, a translation,
a new chair, a winter coat, a clever gift,
a friend, or conversation with a friend who's far away,
or simply not right here.

Among the many things she seeks,
may she seek first your kingdom, Lord,
your righteousness,
and may she find all other good and needful things
as blessings added from your gracious hand.

So many harmful or distracting or unnecessary things
we restless humans seek in cyberspace,
where prowling evil often hides behind a pleasing face
that captures one who just steps closer in to see.
Guard her, O Lord; deliver her from evil—
whether numbing little steps away from what is good,
or evil willfully embraced, rebellion outright.

Work in her, Father, by your Holy Spirit,
drawing her to seek your kingdom
and your righteous King, your Son, our Savior
who has washed away our sin and given us his righteousness.

May you rule over all the places, people, things she seeks
inside, outside her door—or in some virtual space;
may she keep seeking first your kingdom,
where, with you, is every thing she needs.

My son, do not lose sight of these—
  keep sound wisdom and discretion,
and they will be life for your soul
  and adornment for your neck.
Then you will walk on your way securely,
  and your foot will not stumble.
If you lie down, you will not be afraid;
  when you lie down, your sleep will be sweet. (Prov. 3:21–24)

How good to pray for our children's rest! (We can't help but
be praying for our own rest as well.) And how important—not
just that their bodies would be healthy and refreshed by regular, deep, peaceful sleep, but also that their souls would be at
rest, at peace with God through the Lord Jesus Christ and the
ministry of the Spirit.

Our grown children do not go alone into their days and
nights. What a comfort to commit them to the Lord who does
not slumber or sleep (see Ps. 121:4).

For Nighttime Rest

May he know the rest of one who labors well and wisely,
having aimed in hours of light to please you, Lord,
then resting in the hours of night as one who knows his way
along the path you put before him,
going before him night and day
and by your Spirit showing him the way.

I pray he would embrace the rhythm of dark and light,
of sleep renewing and of morning zest.
When he lies down, would you make his sleep sweet?
May evening prayers seep into dreams
that would not haunt or frighten—
comfort, rather; gladden; or pass harmless by.
And if he wakes, Lord,
may he know you with him,
there to lighten the dark watches of the night
with echoing sustenance of the Word
and comfort from the saving love of Christ
and songs that sweeten all the shadows
'til the morning sends the dark away.

Now, Lord, I do admit,
I'm praying for my rest as well—
so let me rest
in offering this prayer to you.

When he established the heavens, I was there;
* when he drew a circle on the face of the deep,*
when he made firm the skies above,
* when he established the fountains of the deep,*
when he assigned to the sea its limit,
* so that the waters might not transgress his command,*
when he marked out the foundations of the earth,
* then I was beside him, like a master workman,*
and I was daily his delight,
* rejoicing before him always,*
rejoicing in his inhabited world
* and delighting in the children of man. (Prov. 8:27–31)*

In their study and work and leisure and all that fills the lives of young adults, may they enjoy creativity—creativity developed and expressed using their unique, God-given gifts, and creativity that honors our Creator.

One young man in our church works in business during the week and plays the cello in our worship services on the weekends. His creativity certainly enriches our church life, and I'm sure it enriches his work life and his personal life as well.

The Bible teaches us to celebrate God's creation—and shows us how God delights in what he creates. May our children carry on this celebration and delight, in all that they do.

The Word from the beginning: see John 1:1–3.

For Holy Creativity

In all her work and all her making, Lord—
a song, an essay, or a loaf of bread—
let her remember to delight in you her Maker,
to rejoice in all that you have made,
and to be mindful that her making is a gift from you
who made the earth and seas, shaping and bounding them
according to your word and with immeasurable joy.

In all her care and creativity in learning, Lord,
let her remember to adore your Son,
the Word from the beginning there with you,
your master workman
by whom everything was made
and in whom you delight.
In him may she rejoice; in him may she know your delight.

In all her dreams of making something new,
let her remember to depend on Jesus's saving work
upon the cross, where sin was paid for,
brokenness all healed, new life given free
in our Redeemer who makes all things new
for those who trust in him
and who then spread his life, in every moment's shaping.

Make her a maker in whom you delight, O Father God,
like Jesus Christ your master workman at creation.
May all she makes bring glory to her Maker,
praise to her Redeemer,
lasting joy to her, a joy reflecting all that you have made.

Blessed is the man
  who walks not in the counsel of the wicked,
nor stands in the way of sinners,
  nor sits in the seat of scoffers;
but his delight is in the law of the LORD,
  and on his law he meditates day and night. (Ps. 1:1–2)

Another prayer about the Word of God . . . because there is hardly anything more central to pray for. Our child's heart for the Scriptures affects all these other matters we're praying about. That verse I learned many years ago from the King James Version tells the truth: "Thy word have I hid in mine heart, that I might not sin against thee" (Ps. 119:11).

Of course, we're not talking about just head knowledge of true facts but a personal knowledge of the personal Lord who breathed out these words. We're talking about knowing and loving the Lord Jesus who shines through these words from beginning to end.

And so we pray that our children would not only learn the Word but also *meditate* on it day and night.

Life-giving breath: see 2 Timothy 3:16.

For Word-Shaped Thoughts

Day and night, Lord, day and night until there is no night,
please let him meditate upon your Word.

Let him be muttering and musing on a phrase
that puzzles or delights him—
and may that life-giving breath from you
expel the impure thoughts that would invade his mind.

Let him be practicing the joy
of speaking the psalms' prayers and praises—
and may those routes traced deep within
direct the lifelong travels of his soul.

May he dig deep into the prophets' words,
as your own Spirit leads him to see meaning
both for the ones who listened first
and now for him, as he sees Jesus clearly.

Let him be savoring Scripture's solid teaching,
laboring through the gospel logic of the apostle Paul;
filled with such food may he walk day by day
away from empty words and acts, toward what is good and true.

Day and night, Lord, day and night until there is no night,
please let him meditate upon your Word.

The steadfast love of the LORD never ceases;
*   his mercies never come to an end;*
they are new every morning;
*   great is your faithfulness.*
"The LORD is my portion," says my soul,
*   "therefore I will hope in him." (Lam. 3:22–24)*

What a comfort for parents, even when we cannot understand or fix whatever inner struggle our children are experiencing, to be able to pray and ask God's help for them.

We can tell our grown children of God's faithfulness to us in times of darkness of soul. We can share the Word with them. We can be quiet with them. We can help them in practical ways with words and acts of kindness. We can encourage them to seek the wisdom and fellowship of God's people in the local church family. Most important, we can pray. First and last and over and over, we can take our children to the Lord in prayer.

For Hope in Trouble

Don't let her stay in the dark of night, dear Lord;
please bring to mind and heart your mercies
that are new each morning. May she know
and hope in your great faithfulness.

When what she hoped for fails—
a plan undone, a friendship severed—
may she consider you to be her portion;
may she hope in you.

If she begins to doubt herself,
her strength, her adequacy for a task ahead,
may she not give in to dark and fearful thoughts,
but may she give herself to you, O God of hope.

Let her remember how our Savior
came and suffered in our place upon that cross,
drinking the bitterest cup, of your own wrath,
so that we never must descend to depths of hell.

And may she think of how he rose from that dark grave,
and how, in him, we have new life
and resurrection life to come, forever.
May hope in you, dear Lord, turn night to light.

Do not rebuke an older man but encourage him as you would a father, younger men as brothers, older women as mothers, younger women as sisters, in all purity. (1 Tim. 5:1–2)

When you're young, sometimes you don't know how much you need older people. I can remember not knowing that.

I love these words from the apostle Paul to young Pastor Timothy, offering perspective on Timothy's relationship to the different age groups of men and women in his congregation. All believers can learn from such a perspective as we hear this call to notice, value, and encourage God's people around us, including the older ones.

As we become the older ones, we get to be "prayer warriors" on behalf of the young people around us. What a privileged and blessed position among God's people!

For Honoring Older Saints

Please help him place himself among your people, Lord,
as you ordain our lives together—younger, older,
oldest—those who've seen a myriad of days
and who can help us glimpse the flow
that leads ahead to you.

Let him be close enough to see the veiny skin,
to hear the voices that sound somewhat far away
but that speak words we need to hear,
so that we ponder, learn, lament, or laugh
with mothers and with fathers all around.

Among your family, Lord, please let him plant himself,
especially as he pursues your callings near and far;
may he, while stretching wide his field of vision,
keep secure those roots that bind him to your people
young and old, one body heading for your heavenly home.

As he becomes adept with words
that comment on the world or aim to teach some wisdom,
let him pause to listen well
to voices of the older wise ones,
who have seen the sun rising and falling on so many words.

Let him seek and treasure love and prayers
of faithful mothers, fathers in the faith,
who've persevered and fought the battle well,
and who now know they're called to intercede
for generations rising up to carry it on, all by your grace.

Let no one despise you for your youth, but set the believers an example in speech, in conduct, in love, in faith, in purity. (1 Tim. 4:12)

Again we hear Paul speaking to Timothy, encouraging him to "step up" even in his youth, to the point of offering a godly example before the whole congregation. This counsel can speak not just to pastors but also to all believing young people, challenging them to lives of holiness in service to the God who mercifully saved them through his Son.

In many wars throughout history, so many young people have stepped up and served in amazing ways—leading troops, flying planes into enemy fire, risking their lives with remarkable courage. In our ongoing spiritual battles, may it be the same.

We can expectantly pray for mature, godly lives in Christian young people. When they fail, as we all do, we can look for repentance and change. But let's pray for growth, much good fruit, and godliness that sets an example for all of us.

For Service and Ministry

Let her not hesitate to give herself in service—
as a servant first of all to you, our Lord;
may she be ready, humbly, unreservedly,
to walk as one who's called by you to serve.

May her speech strengthen and encourage,
as her words echo your Word,
chosen with restraint
and helping those around her turn to you.

May her conduct be pleasing in your eyes,
with private actions matching public view,
and Spirit-led self-control
keeping her steps aligned with Christ her Savior.

May love dwell in her, love from you
and love for you and for your people—
love that overflows and draws in strangers,
aliens, wanderers, those who need your love.

May growing faith sustain her, your great gift
of seeing what's invisible, hoping in the great reality
of you, who sent your Son to save us from our sins.
And may her faith be shared, as she speaks faithfully your Word.

May purity define her mind and soul and body;
may she devote herself to you, to love you all her days—
and even now, in days of youth,
please let her live to serve you.

Let marriage be held in honor among all, and let the marriage bed be undefiled, for God will judge the sexually immoral and adulterous. (Heb. 13:4)

We cannot look ahead and know if God has ordained the gift of marriage for our children. But we can pray that they would honor marriage, whether they find themselves married or not. We are surrounded today by many voices rejecting marriage as a gift from God to be received by a man and a woman as husband and wife. All God's people must bear witness to the goodness of this relationship that so directly pictures his love for his people.

And, yes, I think we can ask God for this gift for our child. Sometimes that prayer lasts many years. Sometimes the answer is no, because God has other good plans. Always the prayer is lifted up to a sovereign, loving Father God whom we can trust fully and forever.

A man and wife together showing forth: see Ephesians 5:31–32.

For Honoring Marriage

Creator God, I pray my child would praise you
for your glory in creation,
with a man and woman as the culmination
of your making—human beings, in your image,
male and female, man and wife, in perfect union.

If he marries, and if he does not,
give him, Lord, clear eyes to see the glorious good
of your creation plan—a man and wife
together showing forth the mystery profound
of Christ and his beloved church, for whom he died.
Please let him honor marriage, as he honors you;
may he be quick to celebrate its goodness,
to stand firm against what breaks it down,
to rejoice with those who know its joys,
to grieve with those who suffer when it's marred by sin.

Let him walk the path of wisdom toward his marriage,
should you ordain for him this gift;
may he not rush to claim it—or set the gift aside,
consumed by other goods he judges urgent.
May he look deep into the wonder of your Son and of your
        church;
let him long to love and live out such a wonder.
Let him learn to love according to your Spirit and your Word.
Would you prepare for him another longing, loving heart
as you began to do in Eden?

This I pray, full knowing that your plans are good and glorious,
from the beginning given to honor your glorious Son.

Have this mind among yourselves, which is yours in Christ Jesus, who, though he was in the form of God, did not count equality with God a thing to be grasped, but emptied himself, by taking the form of a servant, being born in the likeness of men. And being found in human form, he humbled himself by becoming obedient to the point of death, even death on a cross. Therefore God has highly exalted him and bestowed on him the name that is above every name, so that at the name of Jesus every knee should bow, in heaven and on earth and under the earth, and every tongue confess that Jesus Christ is Lord, to the glory of God the Father. (Phil. 2:5–11)

We, and our children, and all human beings, are heading toward that moment when we will see Jesus face to face—Jesus, the Son of God, the Savior who came in the flesh and died, the risen and glorious Lord, the judge of all, the Redeemer who will live and reign with his people forever.

As our children walk their pathways, may they trust God's salvation for them in the Lord Jesus Christ. By God's grace, may they follow Jesus until they see his glorious face.

Who from the beginning was with God: see John 1:1–2.

For My Child to Think on Jesus

As my child walks on, finding her way,
may all her thoughts be full of Jesus.

May she think on Jesus Christ the Son of God
who from the beginning was with God,
was God, dwelling in heaven's glory.
Thinking on the eternal Son, may she wonder at his majesty.

May she think on Jesus who came down from heaven,
obeying perfectly his Father—making himself nothing,
humbling himself, to death, upon a cross.
Thinking on him crucified, may she love and adore the Savior.

May she think on Jesus whom God raised,
whom God exalted high above all names,
that every knee should bow before the name of Jesus.
Thinking on him reigning, may she worship Christ the Lord.

May all her thoughts of Jesus guide her steps.
May Jesus's majesty expand her vision and enlarge her heart.
May Jesus's death upon the cross be her salvation and her song.
May Jesus's reign and imminent return give shape to all her
        plans.

As my child walks on, finding her way,
may all her thoughts be full of Jesus.

For this reason I bow my knees before the Father, from whom every family in heaven and on earth is named. (Eph. 3:14–15)

The "reason" for Paul's prayer in Ephesians 3 is the glorious truth of God's redemptive plan to create a people for himself from all the nations of the earth through his Son. In light of this magnificent truth, Paul brings his praises and petitions to God who is the ultimate *Father*, the only source of life and true identity for human beings as we come to him through his Son.

As parents we pray to God the glorious Father of us all. In allowing us to parent children, God is showing us himself and drawing us to himself. May we learn about our heavenly Father and show off our heavenly Father as we treasure the gift of parenting. May our parenting be to our Father's glory.

For My Parent Heart

O Father God, you know my parent heart.
You are the heavenly parent
who has let your children taste
the joy and care
of fathering and mothering,
so opening your self—
if we would see—
to show the depths of your delight
in what you make.

So let me never set my eyes
on caring for my parent heart
or on a child as my end,
but let me look to see
you, Lord, who made us,
gave us life and life ongoing
through your Son,
all for your glory alone.

May all these prayers be to that end,
that you, O Father God,
through this my parent heart,
and through my child,
might show your Father-love,
revealed to us in Christ your Son,
and overflowing through your Spirit,
for the glory of your name.

Soli Deo gloria.

Conclusion

Raising children is one continual process of learning to let them go. That is one way to say it—although it might not be the best way. I recall a scene from a movie in which an astronaut in space was floating and exploring outside his spaceship, dressed in his spacesuit and tethered securely to his ship. Suddenly the tether broke, and he just floated away into outer space, lost forever.

Letting our children go is not like that! We can so easily get the picture wrong in our minds. We parents are not the safe place, and the tether must not attach to us.

Psalm 37:5 helps us think rightly: "Commit your way to the LORD; trust in him, and he will act." My Bible concordance tells me that the word *commit* in that verse means literally "to roll," as in rolling a large stone. When we roll something, we're aiming in a certain direction, heading for a particular place. To commit our way—or our children—to the Lord is not to let them float away; it is to roll them into the hands of the Lord.

That's a much better way to say it. We Christian parents don't just let go; we purposely commit our children, from the start, into the hands of God—the only safe place. We pray they will be tethered to him, through the Lord Jesus. I hope these prayers will be an ongoing help, to that end. Perhaps you will want to write your own prayers in the following blank pages as you "roll" your young adult children into God's hands.

Prayers of a Parent

Did you enjoy this book?
Consider leaving a review online.
The author appreciates your feedback!

Or write to P&R at editorial@prpbooks.com
with your comments. We'd love to hear from you.